MW01251330

**Working With Words**

# Spelling Skills
## for Active Learning

### Irene Yates

Pembroke Publishers Limited

Pembroke Publishers Limited
538 Hood Road
Markham, Ontario L3R 3K9 Canada
1-800-997-9807

Distributed in the U.S. by Stenhouse Publishers
431 York Street, York, Maine 03909
1-800-988-9812

**Canadian Cataloguing in Publication Data**

Yates, Irene
  Spelling skills for active learning

(Working with words)
Includes index.
ISBN 1-55138-094-3

1. English language — Orthography and spelling — Study and teaching
(Elementary). I. Title. II. Series: Yates, Irene. Working with words

LB1574.Y37 1998        372.63'2044        C98-931648-3


Editor:              Cynthia Young
Cover Design:        John Zehethofer
Illustrations:       Kate Ford
Typesetting:         Jay Tee Graphics Ltd.


Printed and Bound in Canada
9 8 7 6 5 4 3 2 1

# Contents

# Introduction

Strong visual perception, visual memory and recall, well-developed auditory discrimination and auditory memory are necessary for good spelling.

Positive and practical encouragement, workable strategies and systematic teaching will develop these skills in all children. In turn, the skills will lead them towards spelling confidence.

There is a proven link between handwriting and spelling. A child is helped to spell a word correctly when the handwriting flows. Cursive writing is much more valuable for spelling than printing where the child forms each letter separately, taking the pencil from the paper for each one. Regular handwriting lessons will help children with letter sequencing.

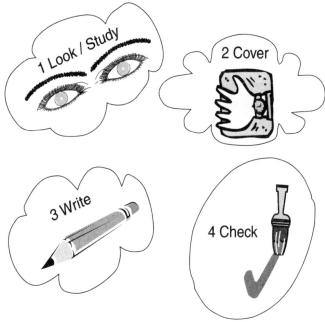

"Copying" a word is not a good idea since children tend to look at a letter, write it, then go back to look at the next letter, write that, go back to look at the next, etc. It is much better to break the word into syllables or clusters of letters and write each one as a unit, covering the original word. In this way the child will develop visual/auditory memory and recall.

A planned and structured course of spelling instruction can stimulate children's interest in language and how it works. They are often intrigued by the origins of words and the reasons why they are spelled the way they are. This kind of information helps them, in turn, to become confident and positive spellers.

# Spelling Skills Inventory

| **Spelling and Vocabulary Skills** | Page References |
|---|---|
| • use sound-symbol relationships (phonics) to help decode, spell, and learn new words | 6, 7, 8, 10, 11, 12, 15, 17, 18, 19, 20, 22, 26, 30, 31, 37, 40, 41, 42, 43 |
| • use structural analysis and word patterns to spell or form familiar and new words, and to learn new vocabulary | 10, 13, 18, 19, 20, 21, 22, 23, 24, 25, 30, 31, 32, 33, 34, 35, 36, 39 |
| — divide words into syllables | 8, 9 |
| — apply conventional spelling rules | 16, 17, 18, 20, 21, 22, 23, 24, 25, 26, 30, 31, 38, 39, 40, 41, 42 |
| — know and use common exceptions to conventional spellings | 19, 22, 24, 31, 40, 41 |
| — use root words and suffixes to form plurals, tenses and word endings | 23, 25, 34, 35, 36, 39 |
| — use root words and prefixes to form new and/or compound words | 20 |
| • know and use familiar homophones and homonyms | 27, 28, 29 |
| • form contractions correctly | 38 |
| • use spelling tools to learn and spell specialized terminology | 9, 10, 11, 12, 13, 14, 15 |
| • proof read materials before submitting final copy | 16 |

| **Grammar Skills** | |
|---|---|
| • understand and use a variety of sentence structures (e.g., simple, compound, complex sentences; statements, questions, exclamations) | 8 |
| • understand and use clauses correctly in sentences | 8, 14, 18 |

# Learn the vowels

Five of the letters in the alphabet are called vowels. They are the ones you sound in your throat with your mouth open. You need to learn the vowels off by heart. There are only five, so it's not hard work. They are:

<table>
<tr><td>a</td><td>e</td><td>i</td><td>o</td><td>u</td></tr>
</table>

Fill in the palm tree trunks with three or four letter words that contain one or more of the vowels. Go for twelve words for each vowel. Your words can be as easy or as difficult as you choose.

**Tip:** Copying the letters of words one or two at a time won't make you a good speller. You need to practise seeing the whole word in your mind's eye.

**EXTRA!**
Sometimes, but not often, we use the letter "y" in place of "i" as a vowel.
For example: rhythm. Make a collection of these words on a page in your word book.

# Learn the consonants

There are 26 letters of the alphabet. Five are vowels, so that leaves 21 consonants. Consonants are the sounds made by making different shapes with your lips and tongue.

Write the consonants in alphabetical order in the comet heads.

Write two words for each letter in the comet tails – the consonant can be the initial letter or be a letter within the word. Try to make them words you would use in your writing. Check your words in a dictionary. Circle any words you've had trouble with.

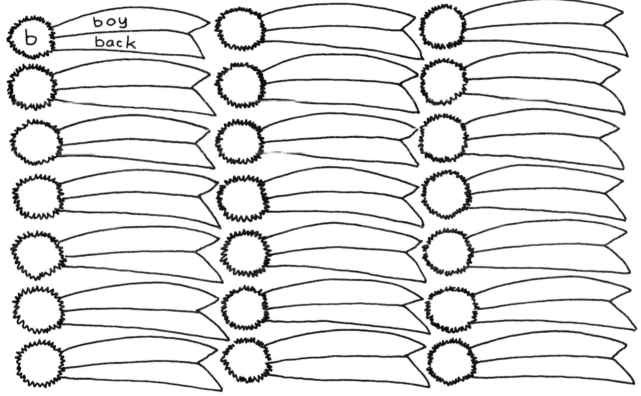

Choose no more than five words you would like to learn. Write them here:

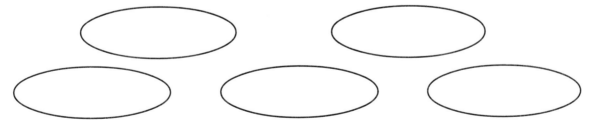

---

**EXTRA!**
Try to fix a picture of the five words in your head. Write a first draft of a short poem or story using the words. Check them again.

---

*Spelling Skills for Active Learning*
Pembroke Publishers

# Sound bites

Words break into sound units, or beats, which are called "syllables." You need to sound words aloud to find out how many syllables they have. Remember you're to think about how they sound, not how they look.

**Tip:** Every syllable contains at least one vowel.

For example:
When nine thousand aliens landed in the school playground, our teacher went wild.

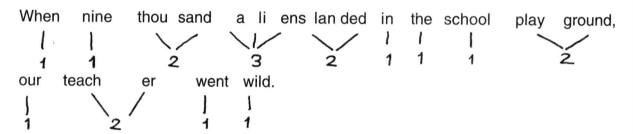

Write four more sentences to this story and then work out the number of syllables in each of your words.

*Breaking words into syllables will help you to work out how to spell them.*

Count the number of words with 1, 2, 3 or 4 syllables and fill in this chart:

| Words with 1 syllable | Words with 2 syllables | Words with 3 syllables | Words with 4 syllables |
|---|---|---|---|
|  |  |  |  |

*A Spelling Haiku*

*Spelling isn't hard,*
*Once you know some of the tricks.*
*That makes it easy.*

**EXTRA!**
Write some Haiku poems. A Haiku has three lines:
Line 1   =   5 syllables
Line 2   =   7 syllables
Line 3   =   5 syllables

*Spelling Skills for Active Learning*
Pembroke Publishers

# The four-step method

The four-step method to learning how to spell a word is:

1 Look / Study   2 Cover   3 Write   4 Check

1   You need to learn to **look** – it's no good just flicking your eyes across the word. Break it into syllables in your head. Study the word for letter patterns. Look for any tricky bits and concentrate on getting a picture of them in your mind's eye.

2   **Cover** the word and say it aloud.

3   **Write** the word. Say it as you write it.

4   **Check** if you've got the word right. If not, write the *whole* word again, not just part of it.

Have a go at these words:

| Look/study | Cover and write | Check and write correctly | Repeat next day |
|---|---|---|---|
| planet<br>extra-terrestrial<br>alien<br>intergalactic<br>spaceship<br>astronaut<br>weird<br>force<br>flight<br>shuttle<br>dangerous<br>mission | | | |

**EXTRA!**
Write a space adventure story, using as many of these words as you can.

*Spelling Skills for Active Learning*
Pembroke Publishers

# Imaging the words

Make picture images of words you're learning, in your mind's eye.

Try this: Close your eyes. Think of something pleasant. Imagine a sheet of your favorite color. Open your eyes and look at the following word:

Divide the word into syllables like this: PTER-O-SAUR. The "P" isn't pronounced.

## pterosaur

Focus you eyes on it for several seconds. Go from the beginning to the end of it, then from the end to the beginning. Look at the shape of it. Close your eyes again and look at the sheet of your favorite color. Inside you head, without opening your eyes, look upwards and to the left. Imagine writing **pterosaur** on your colored sheet, with a colored pen, and look at it.

Open your eyes – look upwards and to the left as though you were looking at the word on your sheet, then write it here:

Check your spelling.

Choose five words from your writing that you've had problems with, or write five new words that you'd like to learn, and learn them in this way.

1

2

3

4

5

**EXTRA!**
Write an acrostic of the word: pterosaur. (An acrostic is a poem, phrase or sentence in which the first letters form a word.)

# The sound trick

Sound triggers are a good memory trick for spelling. First, study the word that's bothering you. Suppose the word is "friend."

Look at the shape and pattern of the word:

## friend

Work out which is the difficult bit. In "friend" usually it's the "ie" bit. Read the word again and trigger the "ie" off in your mind by reading it as frI-End (pronounce it "FRY-end"). Read the word over and over as frI-end. Cover the word, see it in your mind's eye and say it to yourself. Now open your eyes and write the word here:

Another example: beautiful. The hard bit is "eau." Read it as b-E-A-U-tiful (say b-EE-AY-YOO-tiful). Practise learning it as before, then write it.

Make your own sound triggers for these awkward words:

| word | sound trigger | cover and have a go |
|---|---|---|
| science | | |
| said | | |
| when | | |
| why | | |
| calf | | |
| comb | | |
| fight | | |
| bought | | |

Use this learning method, then test yourself on the words. Get a friend to test you the next day.

---

**EXTRA!**

Try to find out what your most common mistakes are. If you find you have trouble with words beginning with "wh," learn them as w-hen, w-here, w-hy.
If you have trouble with not hearing "n" sounds, learn the words as beloNg, siNk, grouNd.

---

*Spelling Skills for Active Learning*
Pembroke Publishers

# The picture trick

Picture tricks help you to remember. The picture is in your mind and doesn't have to make sense to anyone else.

First, study a word that's bothering you.

Suppose that word is "disappear." Look at the shape and pattern of the word:

disappear

Work out the difficult bit. It's usually trying to remember that there is one "s" and two "p"s. Think of a squirrel for the "s" and two pinecones for the "p"s. In your mind's eye, watch a door open in a tree and the squirrel with its two pinecones disappear into it. Hey presto – one "s" and two "p"s – disappear! The sillier your picture clue is, the more it will help you to remember.

Another example: bicycle **bicycle**

Make a list of six words you find difficult. Illustrate them with silly picture clues that will help you to remember them. Learn the words by seeing them together with your pictures in your mind.

**Tip:** Concentrate on learning just three words at a time.

| Write your words here | Picture clues | Cover and try |
|---|---|---|
|  |  |  |

---

**EXTRA!**

Test yourself after your study. Score 2 points for every word you get right.
Get a friend to test you tomorrow. Score 3 points for every word you get right.

Practise, then ask your friend to test you again in a week's time. Score 5 points for every word you get right. This gives a possible score of 60 points.

*Spelling Skills for Active Learning*
Pembroke Publishers

# The acrostic trick

You can learn difficult words by inventing acrostics. An acrostic is a poem, phrase, or sentence where the initial letters of each line make up your word.

Suppose your word is:     hear

Write the letters down the page. You might remember how to spell it with this acrostic:

> **h** appiness is
> **e** very day, having
> **a** ll my friends
> **r** ound to play.

> Your acrostics don't have to rhyme.

Another example:    when

> **w** e
> **h** ave
> **e** arly
> **n** ights when we're at school.

When you've written your acrostic, memorize it by closing your eyes and writing it in your head. When you want to recall the word, just recall your acrostic and write down the initial letters of each line.

Choose six words you need to learn, then work out acrostics for them.
(You could work with a friend.)

**EXTRA!**
Recite your acrostics to a friend and get them to work out what your words are and how to spell them correctly.

*Spelling Skills for Active Learning*
Pembroke Publishers

# The silly sentence trick

> The sillier your sentences are, the more likely you are to remember them.

Create a sentence using each letter as the first letter of a word. You must keep them in the right order!

For instance: TOGETHER
**T**wo **O**ld **G**reen **E**xtra **T**errestrials **H**ad **E**xploding **R**ockets.

Write sentences for these words:

| Words | Sentences | Cover and try |
|---|---|---|
| SCIENCE | | |
| MAGNETIC | | |
| PICTURE | | |

Learn your sentences, then test yourself.

Find up to six words you want to learn and use this trick to learn them.

| My words | Sentences | Cover and try |
|---|---|---|
| | | |

## EXTRA!
Choose one of your silly sentences and write a story with it as your opening sentence. Try to use some of the new words you've learned. Check your first draft for words that don't look right.

# Just for fun!

If there's a word that really makes your mind go blank every time you go to write it down, use the alphabet that's used in Radio Communications.

*I think spelling is Bravo Romeo India Lima Lima India Alpha November Tango!*

**The phonetic alphabet**

A = Alpha
B = Bravo
C = Charlie
D = Delta
E = Echo
F = Foxtrot
G = Golf
H = Hotel
I = India

J = Juliet
K = Kilo
L = Lima
M = Mike
N = November
O = Oscar
P = Papa
Q = Quebec
R = Romeo

S = Sierra
T = Tango
U = Uniform
V = Victor
W = Whisky
X = X-ray
Y = Yankee
Z = Zulu

Learn your name and three friends' names in the phonetic alphabet.

| Names | Phonetic alphabet | Cover and try |
|-------|-------------------|---------------|
|       |                   |               |

Choose six words you sometimes spell wrong and write them here in the phonetic alphabet. Learn them, then check.

| Your words | Phonetic alphabet | Cover and try |
|------------|-------------------|---------------|
|            |                   |               |

**EXTRA!**
Find out why it's called the phonetic alphabet.

*Spelling Skills for Active Learning*
Pembroke Publishers

# Spot the mistake!

To be a good speller, get into the habit of "proof reading" your work.

Write your first draft without worrying too much about the spelling. When you get to the end, go back and check like this:

**How to proof read**

1 Use a rule under the line to check each word at a time. Ask yourself if the word looks right.

2 Draw a circle round any word you think you need to check.

3 Ask yourself how else the word could be spelled. Try different ways on scrap paper.

4 Check the spelling with a dictionary, a friend, a computer spell check or an adult.

5 Compare your spelling with the right one and make a note of any part you got wrong.

6 Get someone else to check whether you have circled all the suspect words.

Write a story here. Don't worry about spelling as you write. When you have finished, proof read your story and correct all the spelling mistakes.

Use the back of the sheet if you need more room.

**EXTRA!**
Sometimes it's helpful to act as a proof reader for someone else.
Swap first drafts with a friend or partner and proof read each other's work.

*Spelling Skills for Active Learning*
Pembroke Publishers

# Words that end with "e"

There are different rules for words that end with "e."

**Magic "e"**
A silent "e" at the end of a word makes the vowel in front say its name.

Write the new words you get when you add "e" to these words.

| | | | |
|---|---|---|---|
| rat | rip | not | cut |
| hat | rid | hop | hug |
| mad | plan | pop | tub |
| man | fin | cod | us |
| mat | pin | rod | pip |

*Read the words you have made aloud.*

Hardly any English words end in "u" and "v." When you hear those sounds at the end of the word you know that it will usually end in "e."

Solve these clues:

**Words that end with a "u" sound**
- the opposite of false ( _ _ _ _ )
- you use it to stick things ( _ _ _ _ )
- a color ( _ _ _ _ )
- one of these will help you find the answer ( _ _ _ _ )
- worth the money ( _ _ _ _ _ )

*You should have an "e" in the tinted box for each word.*

**Words that end with a "v" sound**
- hand it over ( _ _ _ _ )
- go to live somewhere else ( _ _ _ _ )
- a number ( _ _ _ _ _ _ )
- not straight ( _ _ _ _ _ )
- go away ( _ _ _ _ _ _ )
- work in a shop ( _ _ _ _ _ )

**Tip:** The sound of "uv" is spelled "ove" – love, dove, above, glove, shove.

**EXTRA!**
An "e" at the end of a word makes "c" say "s" as in "race." Find six words ending in "ce" and write sentences for each.

*Spelling Skills for Active Learning*
Pembroke Publishers

# The "ei" rules

It helps to learn the rules for words that have an "i" and an "e" together.

The general rule is: "i" before "e," unless they come after a "c" – if they do it's "e" before "i."
For example:

Words that have an "i" and an "e" that sound like "ay" have the "e" before the "i." For example:

Words that have "i" and "e" that sounds like "i" have the "e" first. For example:

*"Either" and "neither" are tricky. They can be pronounced in two ways. The "ei" can sound like "i" or "ee."*

Work out the clues to the word puzzle. All the words have an "i" and an "e." Work out which rule they fit into and put them in the right box.

| "i" before "e" | follows a "c" | sounds like "ay" |
|---|---|---|
| | | |

## Clues

- Blood is carried in them (v _ _ ns)
- A bride wears one over her face (v _ _ l)
- Daughter of your uncle (n _ _ ce)
- It's over your head in the house (c _ _ ling)
- Part of armor (sh _ _ ld)
- kings do it (r _ _ gn)

- Somebody who is vain is this (conc _ _ ted)
- Heavy or lightness (w _ _ ght)
- They live next door (n _ _ ghbors)
- If you tell a lie you do this (dec _ _ ve)
- A kind of toboggan (sl _ _ gh)
- A portion or bit of something (p _ _ ce)

---

### EXTRA!
Make a list of all the "ie" and "ei" words on this page. Work with a friend to make up a funny story using as many of the words in it as you possibly can.

---

# Unruly words

Not all "ie" and "ei" words fit any of the rules. The only thing you can do is learn them.

The most common words that don't fit are:

| | | | |
|---|---|---|---|
| their | sovereign | seize | counterfeit |
| forfeit | foreign | leisure | weird |

Find these words in the word search:

| r | f | o | r | e | i | g | n | o | l | w |
|---|---|---|---|---|---|---|---|---|---|---|
| e | r | u | s | y | w | o | r | s | e | o |
| c | o | u | n | t | e | r | f | e | i | t |
| e | v | e | r | b | i | a | c | s | s | s |
| i | z | e | r | y | r | u | o | d | u | e |
| t | h | e | i | r | d | l | o | u | r | i |
| f | o | r | f | e | i | t | n | o | e | z |
| s | o | v | e | r | e | i | g | n | g | e |

List the words you've found here:

---

**EXTRA!**
Make up some sentences using these words to help you remember them.
You could write your sentences as a story.

---

*Spelling Skills for Active Learning*
Pembroke Publishers

# "qu" words

You will never even find a "q" on its own in any English words. It is **always** followed by a "u." "qu" sounds like "kw" (except when in queue and quay) and "qu" is **always** followed by a vowel.

Here is a "qu" word puzzle:

1  The aliens closed their mouths and were qu _ _ _ .
2  The aliens nearly drowned when they tried to join in the _ qu _ sports.
3  Mrs. Jones was pleased to make the aliens' leader's _ _ qu _ _ _ _ _ _ _ _ .
4  The aliens began to qu _ _ _ _ _ about who would write on the chalkboard.
5  They found some parts of the number qu _ _ very difficult.
6  The aliens counted their fingers but couldn't get an _ qu _ _ number.
7  The qu _ _ _ _ _ _ was, what were the aliens going to do next?
8  The classroom was qu _ _ _ _ _ cleared up after they'd left.

Find ten more "qu" words of your own. Use a dictionary to help you. Write a story using all your words.

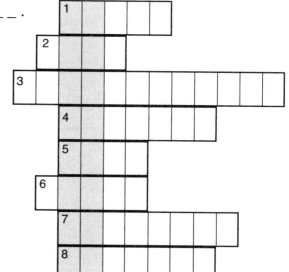

If you've spelled the words correctly, "qu" will appear in the tinted box for each word.

## EXTRA!
Make a collection of "qu" words in your own personal word book. Look for words in your dictionary that begin with "qu" or have "qu" somewhere in them. Note that there are no words that end in "qu."

# Doubles

Some letters like to double themselves if they're in a very short word and follow a vowel.

The letters "l," "f" and "s" are in this group. So, for example, you get:

call                    stiff                    toss

tell                    stuff                    miss

Find ten words for each of these double letters (You can use a dictionary to help you.)

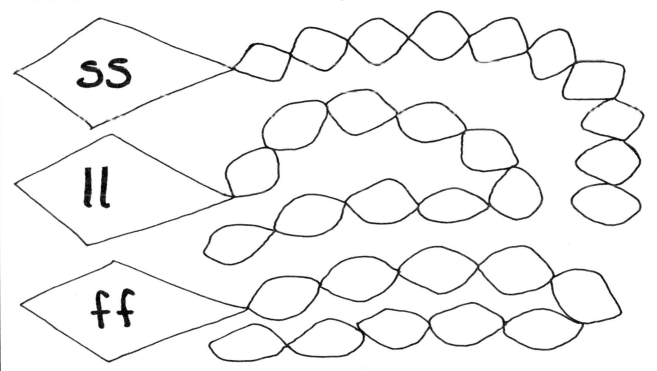

Choose six double letter words and write a poem using them.

**EXTRA!**
There are exceptions to
this rule:
nil, pal, us, bus, gas,
yes, plus, if, of.
Can you find any more?

Use the back of the sheet if you need more room.

*Spelling Skills for Active Learning*
Pembroke Publishers

# "y" for "i" and "ee"

The "ee" sound at the end of a word is nearly always shown as a "y."

Work in groups of four. You each have two minutes to think of as many words as you can that end with the sound of "ee." For example:

    easy          pretty          cheeky          baby

Write your words here. Remember the "ee" sound will usually be a "y."

Each person reads out their list and everyone ticks off his words. Score 1 point for any word nobody else has got. Check the spelling. Score another point for each correct spelling to find the winner.

Watch out for words like macaroni and spaghetti that are not really English words. Also taxi which is really a short form of "taxicab."

## EXTRA!
What about settee, coffee, committee? These are exceptions to the rule. Look through your dictionary and make a list of all the words ending with "ee" that you can find.

# Regular plurals

If a word ends in an "e" — just add "s." The plural of cake is cakes.

Regular plurals are the ones where all you have to do is add an "s."

| Singular | Plural |
|---|---|
| So: one car | three cars |
| one toy | three _____ |
| one elephant | three _____ |

Some words end in a hissing sound when they are plural. Don't be fooled into adding "is." These words have to have an "es" added. These words end in **s**, **x**, **z**, **sh** or **ch**.

| Singular | Plural |
|---|---|
| So: one bus | three buses |
| one fox | three _____ |
| one wish | three _____ |

Make these words plural. Be careful, they're all mixed up!

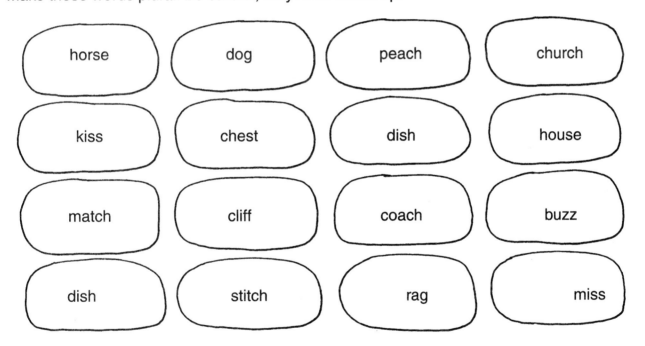

horse    dog    peach    church

kiss    chest    dish    house

match    cliff    coach    buzz

dish    stitch    rag    miss

---

**EXTRA!**
Learn the letters which need "es" to make their plural.
Write as many of these words and their plurals as you can in ten minutes.

*Spelling Skills for Active Learning*
Pembroke Publishers

# Irregular plurals

When a word ends in "f" you have to change the "f" to "ve" before adding the "s" to make it plural.

> **Tip:** Singular means one. Plural means more than one.

Find the singular and plural for these clues.

|  | Singular | Plural |
|---|---|---|

1     a _ _ _ _ of bread

2     a wild animal that hunts in packs ( _ _ _ _ )

3     falls from a tree ( _ _ _ _ )

4     someone who steals ( _ _ _ _ _ )

5     you wear it round your neck ( _ _ _ _ _ )

6     its mother is a cow ( _ _ _ _ )

7     a little creature, in fairy storybooks ( _ _ _ )

8     two quarters equal one _ _ _ _

9     you put books on it ( _ _ _ _ _ )

This one is a bit different. Change the "fe" to "ves" to make it plural.

10     you use it to cut food with ( _ _ _ _ _ )

Some words ending in a consonant plus "o" need "es" added to make them plural. You need to learn which these words are. Write the plurals for these words here:

echo                    hero

mosquito                potato

tomato                  volcano

> **EXTRA!**
> For nouns that end in a consonant followed by "y," change the "y" to "i" and then add "es." For example:
>
> • baby     –     babies
> • story    –     stories
> • fly      –     flies.
>
> If the "y" has a vowel before it, you only need to add an "s." For example:
>
> • key      –     keys
> • monkey   –     monkeys.

# Lose the "l" and gain a word

The words "all," "well," "full" and "till" always lose one "l" when they're added to another word.

For example:

Work out these words:

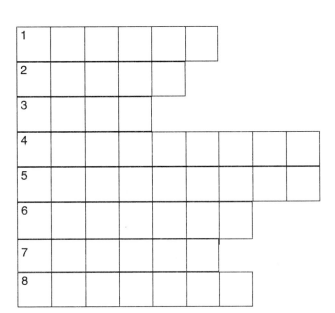

1   Every time (al _ _ _ _ )

2   By myself (al _ _ _ )

3   As well as (al _ _ )

4   Extra specially good ( _ _ _ _ _ _ ful)

5   Very good to look at ( _ _ _ _ _ _ ful)

6   I like to help ( _ _ _ _ ful)

7   Might be of use ( _ _ _ ful)

8   I'm please to see you (wel _ _ _ _ )

Write a poem using these three words. Watch how you spell them!

**almost**          **until**          **awful**

---

**EXTRA!**
Make up a silly sentence or a rhyme, to remind yourself of this spelling rule.

---

*Spelling Skills for Active Learning*
Pembroke Publishers

# Sounds different

The sound "wer" is spelled:     **wor**

| worm | worst | worker | world | work |
| worth | worship | working | word | workplace |

Practise writing the words here. Learn the rule first, then study the words, cover them and write them without looking. Check your spelling. If you get any wrong, spend more time learning them.

> **Tip:** The exception to this rule is the word "were" – as in "we were going to win."

Write a newspaper article using at least six of the words. Check your draft to see if the words look right.

---

### EXTRA!
When you check your spellings:

**Do**
- Circle problem words
- Look for difficult bits
- Write out whole words from memory
- Say each syllable of the word to yourself as you write it.

**Don't**
- Alter bits of words
- Cross out untidily
- Copy words.

# Sounds puzzling

Words that sound exactly the same, but have different meanings and different spellings are called homophones.

whole, hole

You could dig the biggest **hole** in the **whole** world.

bear, bare

A **bear** might attack you when you walk through the forest with **bare** feet.

paws, pause

The wet dog should **pause** at the door to have his **paws** wiped.

**Solve these homophone clues:**

1 • you breathe it ( _ _ _ )
  • something is left to him in a will
    ( _ _ _ _ )

2 • read _ _ _ _ _
  • they let you do something, you're

    _ _ _ _ _ _ _

3 • you did it at dinner yesterday ( _ _ _ )
  • it's a number ( _ _ _ _ _ )

4 • you might bounce it ( _ _ _ _ )
  • you make a lot of noise, crying
    ( _ _ _ _ )

5 • there's sand on it ( _ _ _ _ _ _ )
  • a kind of tree ( _ _ _ _ _ )

6 • you're fed up ( _ _ _ _ _ )
  • you play games on it ( _ _ _ _ _ _ )

Check the answers with a friend and a dictionary.

7 • you stop your bike with it ( _ _ _ _ _ _ )
  • if you drop an egg, it will _ _ _ _ _ _

8 • you have it for breakfast ( _ _ _ _ _ _ _ )
  • you listen to or watch its episodes
    ( _ _ _ _ _ _ )

9 • you pick it in the garden ( _ _ _ _ _ _ _ )
  • you make a cake with it ( _ _ _ _ _ _ )

10 • it's hard to see through it ( _ _ _ _ )
  • the team went mad when the batter

    _ _ _ _ _ _ .

### EXTRA!
Use a dictionary to find the partners of: gate, great, gilt, hair, mail, meat, night, pain, peace, stair, tail, teem, thrown, waist, write, you.
Make up a homophone puzzle for your friend.

*Spelling Skills for Active Learning*
Pembroke Publishers

# Homophones cause trouble!

This set of homophones has three words:

their            there            they're

Remember: homophones sound like the same but look different and have different meanings.

Forget what the words sound like and concentrate on what they look like.

---

**their** – this is a "possessive" – it means "belonging to them." Learn **their** with the other possessive words:

| my | – | my coat |
| your | – | your coat |
| her | – | her coat |
| his | – | his coat |
| its | – | its coat |
| our | – | our coats |
| their | – | their coats |

Write seven sentences here, using each of the possessives.

---

**they're** – this always means they are.

| They're going … | = | They are going … |
| They're having … | = | They are having … |
| They're telling … | = | They are telling … |

Write six sentences using **they're**.

**there** – tells you *where* something is and it is used with "is," "are," "was" and "were."

Make up six sentences beginning with either:
- there is …
- there are …
- there was …
- there were…

---

**EXTRA!**
Make up a word search for each of the words, using them ten times each.

# Puzzling w-words

These words are homophones. They *sound* almost the same but each word means something very different.

> We're visiting the place where we were on holiday last year!

we're                were                where

Learn each word by itself so that you get its meaning and the look of it firmly fixed in your mind.

---

**we're** =      we are

We're is a *contraction*. Notice the apostrophe. It goes where you have left out the "a."

Learn **we're** with these other contractions:

| | | |
|---|---|---|
| I'm | = | I am |
| he's | = | he is |
| she's | = | she is |
| you're | = | your are |
| they're | = | they are |

Write one sentence for each of the other contractions and three sentences for **we're**.

---

**where** means a place.

Notice that after the "w" you have "here." Say to yourself:

> "Where? Here. Where? Here. Where? Here."

until you are sure you have learned how to spell **where**.

---

**were** is the past tense of "are."

You use were when you say, or write, phrases such as:
- we were going
- we were happy

Write six sentences for **were**.

---

### EXTRA!
"Wear" and "weir" are also homophones for these words. "Wear" is what you do with clothes, a "weir" is a dam on a river. Create a picture or word game to help you remember their spellings.

---

*Spelling Skills for Active Learning*
Pembroke Publishers

# "ight" words

The "ight" in words such as **sight** and **bright** always sounds like "ite."

Learn "ight" – draw an outline of its shape.

See, hear and feel the shape and order of letters in the cluster sound "ight" by writing it in each of the speech bubbles in a different color or with a different style of lettering.

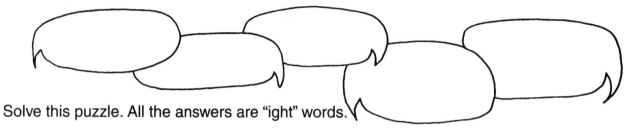

Solve this puzzle. All the answers are "ight" words.

## Across
2  stars are sometimes this
6  this means you're not wrong
7  not heavy – and not dark!
10  don't get into one of these at playtime
11  you could if you wanted – or it could be power
13  roses get it
14  Sir Galahad was one

## Down
1  one of your five senses
3  not loose
4  when owls go hunting
5  a difficult situation
8  get a scare
9  not very big or heavy
12  a bird has the power of this – so does a plane

---

**EXTRA!**
Choose six "ight" words from the puzzle and use them to write an adventure story.

# The "ough" pattern

There are lots of words in English that use the pattern "ough" – but they don't always sound the same.

Learn "ough" – the easiest way is probably to say to yourself **ough** as you write the letters and watch yourself writing them. Write the "ough" pattern in five different styles of writing here:

You can make the sound of "ough" in seven different ways

For example:

The answers to the following puzzle are all "ough" words – you should now know that you'll spell them correctly each time you write them!

| | Clue | Number of letters | The word is | Rhymes with |
|---|---|---|---|---|
| 1 | It isn't smooth | 5 | rough | fluff |
| 2 | It's strong | 5 | | |
| 3 | Got from a shop | 6 | | |
| 4 | An idea | 7 | | |
| 5 | Had a fight | 6 | | |
| 6 | Clear your throat | 5 | | |
| 7 | Pigs eat from it | 6 | | |
| 8 | A tree branch | 5 | | |
| 9 | Used to make bread | 5 | | |
| 10 | In spite of | 6 | | |
| 11 | Go from end to end | 7 | | |
| 12 | Hic! | 8 | | |

## EXTRA!
Practise writing the "ough" pattern in five styles of writing.
Make up your own "ough" quiz and swap it with a friend.

*Spelling Skills for Active Learning*
Pembroke Publishers

# Patterns in words

Always look for patterns of letters in the words you're learning to spell. Patterns are small groups of letters that often appear together, for example:

 th      ck      oa

Get used to spotting them when you're trying to learn new words, or when you're reading.

Look for patterns in these words. Use different colored pencils to color the patterns you find.

| | | | | |
|---|---|---|---|---|
| cockatoo | sheaf | deck | clock | duck |
| teacher | peck | trick | bunch | knuckle |
| pack | jacket | coat | chart | ache |
| check | such | church | ditch | rich |
| clutch | moan | cherry | boast | weak |
| goal | which | butcher | throat | match |
| twitch | watch | gear | grease | loaf |
| goat | pitch | catch | wicked | load |
| hutch | moat | boat | peach | pocket |
| deaf | tea | deaf | witch | kitchen |

Give these five columns headings to match the patterns you've found. Then write the words in the column you think they fit.

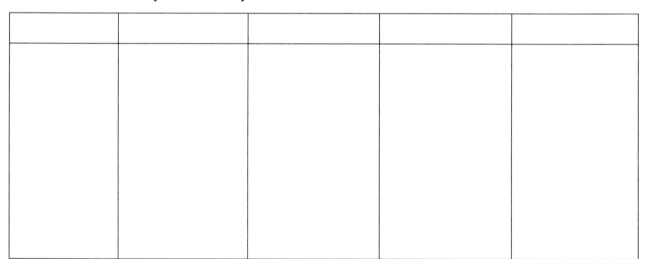

**EXTRA!**
Practise writing these and other letter patterns in joined up writing.
This will help you to remember the correct way to spell them.

# Prefixes

Prefixes are bits which are added to the beginning of words, to make new words. For example:

| Prefix | | Root word | | New word |
|--------|---|-----------|---|----------|
| pre | + | record | = | prerecord |
| un | + | natural | = | unnatural |
| dis | + | appear | = | disappear |

Can you put prefixes on these words to change their meanings? Write the words you make in the boxes.

"pre" means before, so "prefix" = "fix it before."

If the last letter of a prefix is the same as the first letter of the root word, your new word will have a double letter.

| satisfy | comfortable | expected |
|---------|-------------|----------|
| happy | obey | quiet |
| opened | qualify | caution |
| employed | solve | organize |
| grace | arrange | determine |
| historic | judge | position |
| occupied | concerned | suppose |

| pre | un | dis |
|-----|----|----|
| | | |

## EXTRA!
There are other prefixes, such as: "anti," "mis," "auto," "in," "sub," "super," "trans."
Find four words for each of these prefixes.

*Spelling Skills for Active Learning*
Pembroke Publishers

# It happened last week …

Some words sound as if they end in a "t" when they really end in "ed." It's easy to remember which these words are if you know they are what we call "the past tense of verbs."

The "past tense" means the action happened some time before and the words change like this:

Today I jump  Last week I jumped

Today I paint  Yesterday I _____

Today I cook  Last night I _____

Listen hard. It sounds as if the end of the word is "t" or "id," but the real spelling is always "ed."

Verbs are words that you can say "I" with. For example: I play, I am, I sleep, I paint…

| **Tips**: If there is already an "e" there, just add "d." | If the word ends with "y" you need to change it to "i" before adding "ed." | If the word has a "short" vowel, you have to double the consonant before adding "ed." |
|---|---|---|
| Today I save Last week I save**d** | Today I carry Yesterday I carr**ied** | Today I skip Last night I skip**ped** |

Practise changing these verbs to the past tense and write them in proper sentences:

| | | | | |
|---|---|---|---|---|
| act | care | kick | help | chat |
| clap | want | drop | blame | answer |

**EXTRA!**
Make you own collection of verbs you use in your stories. Change them to the past tense.

# Add a bit on

A suffix is a bit that is added to the end of a root word.
One suffix is "ly."

**Tip:** When you add "ly" to a word ending in "ful," your new word with have a double "l."

Spell the words you get if you add "ly" to the root words in these phrases. The first one is done to show you how.

In a sad way        *sadly*

In a careless way

In a cheerful way

In a quick way

In a slow way

In a mad way

Add "ly" to these root words. Write the whole word each time.

| beautiful *beautifully* | successful | awful |
|---|---|---|
| grateful | hopeful | useful |
| thankful | skilful | |

Sometimes you need to lose the last letter of a word and put an "i" in its place before adding "ly."

noisy       becomes       *noisily*

naughty     becomes

pretty      becomes

crazy       becomes

ready       becomes

happy       becomes

speed       becomes

lazy        becomes

**EXTRA!**
There are many different suffixes. Find root words to which you can add:

ing
able
tion
ment

Make a list of as many new words as you can.

*Spelling Skills for Active Learning*
Pembroke Publishers

# Adding endings

**Tip:** When you are adding a suffix to a word that ends with "y" you sometime have to change the "y" to "i."

Be careful— you don't always drop the "y" when you add "ing." For example: hurry - hurrying.

Examples:

| | | | | | | |
|---|---|---|---|---|---|---|
| carry | – | carr**ies** | | reply | – | repl**ies** |
| | | carr**ied** | | | | rep**lied** |
| baby | – | bab**ies** | | happy | – | happ**ily** |

Make as many new words as you can using these suffixes:

 es    ness    ly    ed    ing

and these root words:

*hurried  hurries  hurrying  hurriedly*

hurry          study          seventy

 study           seventy

easy          lazy          body

happy          bully          story

worry          ferry          scurry

---

**EXTRA!**
Write a sentence for each new word.

---

*Spelling Skills for Active Learning*
Pembroke Publishers

36

© Irene Yates
Teachers may photocopy for classroom use only.

# Trip-up words

There are a few words that seem to wait in hiding to trip you up over and over again. One of those words is "have." The reason people often spell "have" incorrectly is because they don't pronounce it the way it's written.

Because of the way we speak, it often sounds as if the word "have" is "of," especially when it follows words like "should," "could" and "would."

Read these sentences aloud and listen to how *you* say the word **have**:

> Mark should have cleaned his bike.
> The Martians couldn't have landed on the field.
> I would have been there to watch them.
> My Dad would have told me.

Make up four sentences each for:

would have    should have    could have    might have

**EXTRA!**
Have a look through some of your stories and highlight all the times you've made this mistake. Write a story using "could have," "should have," "would have" and "might have." Make up funny clues that will help you to remember them.

*Spelling Skills for Active Learning*
Pembroke Publishers

# Making words shorter

When we talk we often shorten words to make our conversation flow better. We can use these shortened forms of words in our writing, but we must remember:

- to put an apostrophe in place of a lost letter (or letters)
- to write the two words together as if they are one.

The words we make shorter are called *contractions*.

Look closely at these examples. Circle the letter or letters that have been left out:

| | | | | | | |
|---|---|---|---|---|---|---|
| I'm | = | I am | you're | = | you are |
| he's | = | he is | I'd | = | I would |
| doesn't | = | does not | it's | = | it is |

Can you finish this puzzle?

| | |
|---|---|
| would not | = |
| does not | = |
| has not | = |
| we are | = |
| I would | = |
| they have | = |
| they would | = |
| she is | = |
| it is | = |
| how is | = |
| what is | = |
| when is | = |
| where is | = |
| do not | = |
| you have | = |

**Tip:** Don't confuse contractions with possessives. **John's** could mean two different things, depending on how it is used:

- "**John's** coat" means "the coat belonging John" (possessive).
- "**John's** going" is short for "John is going" (contraction).

## EXTRA!
Look for as many possible contractions as you can in a book you are reading. Make a list of them. Check with your teacher that you've got them right.

# Growing from the roots

Some words are called "root" words because other words can grow from them, but the main bit of the words always stays the same. So if you learn how to spell the main bit, or "root," you have a head start in getting the whole word right.

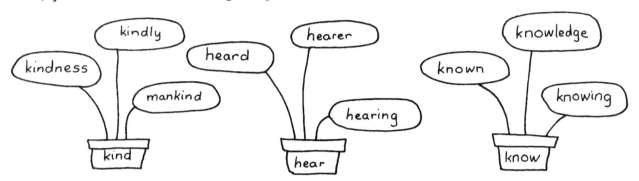

Find the root words for these words.

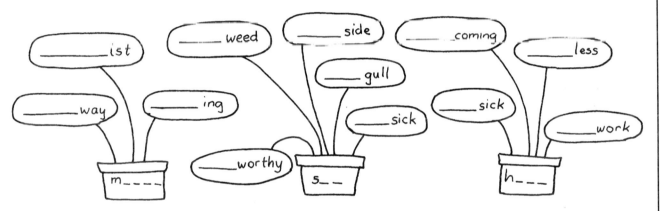

Investigate three root words of your own.

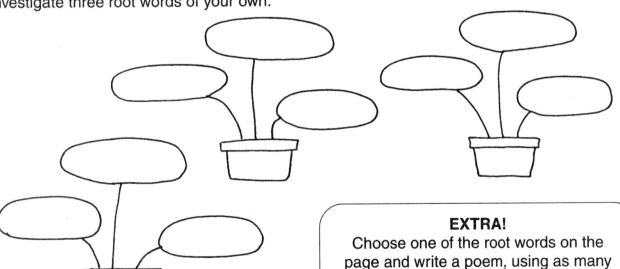

**EXTRA!**
Choose one of the root words on the page and write a poem, using as many forms of the word as you possibly can.

*Spelling Skills for Active Learning*
Pembroke Publishers

# Sssh... k

What has your  got in common with a  ?

A silent "k"!

You say both words as if they begin with an "n."

You can remember silent "k" words by giving yourself a sound clue. In your head make the k-sound at the beginning of the word, so that you get:

k-nee          k-night          k-now

Look in the "kn" section of your dictionary. Make a list here of all the words you can find beginning with a silent "k." Use any method you have learned to help you remember their spelling.

Make up six silly sentences. Try to use an many of the words as possible in each sentence. For example: "The knock-kneed knight kneeled on the knick-knack."

Score 2 points for every new "kn" word you get into each sentence.

## EXTRA!
Work with a friend. Cover your list of words. Dictate your sentences to each other.
Swap papers, uncover your list and mark each other's spellings.
Score 2 points for each "kn" word you get right.

# Don't wake the w!

There are lots of words in the English language that sound as if they should begin with an "r" but they actually begin with a silent "w."

Find the missing silent "w" words for this comic strip.

You've _ _ _ _ _ _ _ that parcel all _ _ _ _ _ _ . Look, the paper is full of _ _ _ _ _ _ _ _ .

Now look what you've done. I _ _ _ _ _ _ my hands of you!

Gran _ _ _ _ _ _ _ _ the parcel off Tommy.

With a flick of Gran's _ _ _ _ _ _ , the parcel _ _ _ _ _ _ _ _ _ free.

Check the words and their spellings with your teacher, friend or dictionary.

Choose six silent letter words of your own and try to work them into your own comic strip.

---

## EXTRA!
There are a few words in English that begin with a silent "g." The silent "g" is always followed by an "n" as in gnome. How many more silent "g" words can you find? Check them with your dictionary. Do the same with the silent "b" at the end of words like "comb."

*Spelling Skills for Active Learning*
Pembroke Publishers

# The silent puzzle

Work out what the words are, then fit them into the grid.

**Tip:** Use a pencil first in case you have to move things around.

## Silent "k"

- something to do with needles ( k _ _ _ )
- if you've learned something you've got this ( k _ _ _ _ _ _ _ _ )
- you need a fork as well ( k _ _ _ _ )
- he wears armor ( k _ _ _ _ _ )
- you do this on a door ( k _ _ _ _ )
- you tie it ( k _ _ _ )

## Silent "w"

- fish do this on a line ( w _ _ _ _ _ _ )
- you wear a watch on it ( w _ _ _ _ )
- not right ( w _ _ _ _ )
- pack up a parcel ( w _ _ _ )

## Silent "b"

- keep you hair tidy ( _ _ _ b )
- don't speak ( _ _ _ b )
- its mother is a ewe ( _ _ _ b )
- feed this to the birds ( _ _ _ _ b )
- on your hand ( _ _ _ _ b )

## Silent "g"

- tiny and bites you ( g _ _ _ )
- old and withered ( g _ _ _ _ _ _ )
- chews ( g _ _ _ _ )
- sits in the garden ( g _ _ _ _ )
- a kind of antelope ( g _ _ )

## Silent "p"

- a flying reptile – what am I? ( p _ _ _ _ _ _ _ _ _ )

**EXTRA!**
Make up a word search for words with special rules, such as:
"i before e" or "magic e." Swap with a friend.

*Spelling Skills for Active Learning*
Pembroke Publishers

# Sounds "ph-unny"!

There are some words that sound as if they begin with an "f," but actually begin with "ph."

Once you get to know which words they are, you will have solved their problem!

| | | |
|---|---|---|
| phantom | philatelist | physics |
| phenomenal | philosopher | phoenix |
| phobia | photocopy | physical |
| phone | photograph | phase |

Draw a circle round any of these words that you know the meaning of. Make a list of an equal number of word beginning with "f." (Check your spelling with a dictionary.)

Write a story here, using as many of the words beginning with "ph" and "f" as you can.

**EXTRA!**
Find out the meaning of the other "ph" words using a dictionary.

*Spelling Skills for Active Learning*
Pembroke Publishers

# You *can* be brilliant at spelling, 1

Spelling isn't always easy because lots of words in the English language are spelled in very funny ways! And that's not the speller's fault!

Some words have "regular" patterns, but lots of words just don't seem to fit any pattern.

You can learn rules and tricks to help you keep hold of the words.

You can also do four things:

- get a picture of the word in your head
- hear the sounds of the word
- understand what the word means
- move your hand/fingers in the exact pattern of the word

**Tips:**
The more of these four things you can do with a new word, the easier you will learn to spell it.

Use your eyes when you're reading. Don't just skim over new words, go back and study them.

Find words to fit these clues:

Six words that have double letters in them

A word that's built up from the root word "easy"

A word beginning with a silent "w"

A word beginning with a silent "k"

Two words that sound the same but have a different spelling (homophones)

A word you didn't know before

A word beginning with "q"

A word you always spell wrong

## EXTRA!
Look through whichever book you're reading and find six words you've never written before. Write them out carefully, then cover and write them again. Check your spelling.

*Spelling Skills for Active Learning*
Pembroke Publishers

# You *can* be brilliant at spelling, 2

There are four links in the chain to being good at spelling. Brilliant spellers know:

- what a word looks like
- what a word sounds like
- how their lips, tongue and hand feel when they say and write the word
- what a word means

This is easy to practise. Start with some simple words. Look at them, "hear" them as you read them in your head and "feel" how your mouth moves as you make the sounds, as well as the pattern your hand makes when you write them.

Work with a friend. On a scrap of paper think of twelve words that one or both of you find difficult to spell. Use a dictionary, a spell checker, or your teacher to help you get them right. Write the words down the left hand side of this paper. Check again that you have spelled them correctly.

Work with three words at a time. Look and say, then write in the columns alongside, saying each word aloud together as you write them. Feel how your hand moves as you write each word.

| Your list | 1st try | 2nd try | 3rd try | 4th try | 5th try |
|-----------|---------|---------|---------|---------|---------|
|           |         |         |         |         |         |
|           |         |         |         |         |         |
|           |         |         |         |         |         |
|           |         |         |         |         |         |

When you have learned the twelve words, turn the pages over and test each other.

**EXTRA!**
Write a sentence for each word. Try to make your sentences read as a story. Check your spelling again.

*Spelling Skills for Active Learning*
Pembroke Publishers

# Answer sheet

**page 17** **words that end with "e"**

| | |
|---|---|
| rate | note |
| hate | hope |
| made | pope |
| mane | code |
| mate | rode |
| ripe | cute |
| ride | huge |
| plane | tube |
| fine | use |
| pine | pipe |

| *words that end with a "u" sound* | *words that end with a "v" sound* |
|---|---|
| true | give |
| glue | move |
| blue | twelve |
| clue | curve |
| value | leave |
| | serve |

**Page 18** **the "ei" rules**

*"i" before "e"*
niece
shield
piece

*follows a "c"*
ceiling
conceited
deceive

*sounds like "ay"*
veins
veil
reign
neighbors
sleigh
weight

**page 20** **"qu" words**
1 quiet
2 aqua
3 acquaintance
4 quarrel
5 quiz
6 equal
7 question
8 quickly

**page 19** **Unruly words**

**page 23** **Regular plurals**

| | |
|---|---|
| toy | toys |
| elephant | elephants |
| fox | foxes |
| wish | wishes |
| horse | horses |
| dog | dogs |
| peach | peaches |
| church | churches |
| kiss | kisses |
| chest | chests |
| dish | dishes |
| house | houses |
| match | matches |
| cliff | cliffs |
| coach | coaches |
| buzz | buzzes |
| dish | dishes |
| stitch | stitches |
| rag | rags |
| miss | misses |

**page 24** **Irregular plurals**

| | | |
|---|---|---|
| 1 | loaf | loaves |
| 2 | wolf | wolves |
| 3 | leaf | leaves |
| 4 | thief | thieves |
| 5 | scarf | scarves |
| 6 | calf | calves |
| 7 | elf | elves |
| 8 | half | halves |
| 9 | shelf | shelves |
| 10 | knife | knives |

**page 24 (continued)**

| | |
|---|---|
| echo | echoes |
| hero | heroes |
| mosquito | mosquitoes |
| potato | potatoes |
| tomato | tomatoes |
| volcano | volcanoes |

**page 25** **Lose the "l" and gain a word**
1 always
2 alone
3 also
4 wonderful
5 beautiful
6 helpful
7 useful
8 welcome

**page 27** **Sounds puzzling**

| | | | | |
|---|---|---|---|---|
| 1 | air | | 6 | bored |
| | heir | | | board |
| 2 | aloud | | 7 | brake |
| | allowed | | | break |
| 3 | ate | | 8 | cereal |
| | eight | | | serial |
| 4 | ball | | 9 | flower |
| | bawl | | | flour |
| 5 | beach | | 10 | mist |
| | beech | | | missed |

# Answer sheet

**page 31    The "ough" pattern**

| | | | |
|---|---|---|---|
| 1 | rough | 7 | trough |
| 2 | tough | 8 | bough |
| 3 | bought | 9 | dough |
| 4 | thought | 10 | though |
| 5 | fought | 11 | through |
| 6 | cough | 12 | hiccough |

**page 34    It happened last week …**

| | |
|---|---|
| paint | painted |
| cook | cooked |
| | |
| act | acted |
| care | cared |
| kick | kicked |
| help | helped |
| chat | chatted |
| clap | clapped |
| want | wanted |
| drop | dropped |
| blame | blamed |
| answer | answered |

**page 35    Add a bit on**

quickly
carelessly
slowly
cheerfully
madly

successfully
awfully
gratefully
hopefully
usefully
thankfully
skilfully

naughtily
prettily
crazily
readily
happily
lazily
speedily

**page 38    Making words shorter**

| | |
|---|---|
| would not | wouldn't |
| does not | doesn't |

**page 30    "ight" words**

**page 42    The silent puzzle**

**Page 38 (continued)**

| | |
|---|---|
| has not | hasn't |
| we are | we're |
| I would | I'd |
| they have | they've |
| they would | they'd |
| she is | she's |
| it is | it's |
| how is | how's |
| what is | what's |
| when is | when's |
| where is | where's |
| do not | don't |
| you have | you've |

**page 41    Don't wake the w!**

You've <u>wrapped</u> that parcel all <u>wrong</u>. Look, the paper is full of <u>wrinkles</u>.

Gran <u>wrenched</u> the parcel off Tommy.

Now look what you've done. I <u>wring</u> my hands of you!

With a flick of Gran's <u>wrist</u>, the parcel <u>wriggled</u> free.

# Glossary

**acrostic**
A poem, phrase or sentence in which the first letters form a word.

**consonant**
A letter that is not a vowel.

**contraction**
A short form of two words.

**device**
An idea to help with learning something.

**exception**
An example that doesn't fit the rules.

**homophone**
A word that has the same sound as another but a different meaning.

**imaging**
Getting a clear mind picture.

**letter patterns**
Sets of letters that appear frequently.

**mnemonics**
A memory aid.

**past tense**
The form of a verb which shows that something happened in the past.

**phonetic**
Representing a sound.

**plural**
More than one.

**prefix**
Added at the beginning of a root word.

**proof read**
Read for errors.

**recall**
Remember.

**root words**
Words which form the base from which other words grow.

**rule**
General principle.

**sentence**
A group of words that make complete sense. Sentences should always have a verb.

**silent letter**
A letter that isn't sounded out.

**singular**
Only one.

**suffix**
Added at the end of a root word.

**syllable**
Unit of a word.

**verb**
A doing or being word.

**vowel**
a, e, i, o, u.

*Spelling Skills for Active Learning*
Pembroke Publishers